What Kind of WAR Was It, Anyhow?

What Kind of WAR Was It, Anyhow?

NANCY EKBERG

ILLUSTRATIONS BY RHONDA REYNOLDS

NEWSOUTH BOOKS

Montgomery

NewSouth Books
105 South Court Street
Montgomery, AL 36104

Library of Congress Cataloging-in-Publication Data
1. United States—History—Civil War, 1861-1865—Juvenile fiction
[1. United States—History—Civil War, 1861–1865—Fiction.]
I. Reynolds, Rhonda, ill. II. Title.
PZ7.E3472Wh 2003
[Fic]—dc21
2003004181

ISBN 978-1-60306-318-0 (paperback)
ISBN 978-1-60306-319-7 (ebook)
ISBN 978-1-58838-085-2 (2003 edition)

Printed in the United States of America

TO
BRETT EKBERG,
WHO ASKED THE QUESTION,
"WHAT KIND OF WAR WAS IT, ANYHOW?"

Dear Reader,

The Civil War was a war fought from 1861 to 1865 between the states of the South, called the Confederacy, and the rest of the states of the United States of America, called the Union.

We all know that slavery was wrong and we realize that if it hadn't been for slavery, there would not have been a Civil War. But most of the men in the South who fought that war did not have slaves. They fought because they did not want the Federal government to make rules about life in the South. Those who fought for the Union forces did not want the South to separate from the Union and divide the country into two nations.

Here is the story of that awful war through the eyes of a boy your age who could have lived then. Jeremy and his family are not real people. But the conditions under which they lived, and the battles and the leaders and the events described in this story are real. Jonathan and Jeremy and Willie and their families are just like many of the families who lived through that war.

— THE AUTHOR

1

Jeremy was ashamed of the tear that was rolling down his cheek. He knew it made him look like a sissy, but he was having a hard time being brave. His best friend and cousin, Jonathan, was going off to be in a war called the Civil War and Jeremy was afraid he wouldn't come back to take him fishing anymore. He couldn't understand why Jonathan wanted to go off and shoot other boys and maybe even get shot himself!

Jeremy was having a lot of trouble understanding this war anyhow.

When he sat at Granddaddy's kitchen table, across the Virginia border in Kentucky, and listened to his kinfolk talk, they said that his uncles and Jonathan were fools to be going off to a war that could break up the United States.

And yet, when he listened to Jonathan and his uncles, here in Virginia where there were plantations, they said the government and President Lincoln had no business telling them how they should run their businesses and plantations and they would sooner leave the United States and set up their own government.

And he got even more confused when he talked to his friend Willie, whose family were slaves on Jeremy's father's tobacco plantation in Virginia. Willie said some of his cousins were going off to fight too, because the war was going to free all of the slaves.

"So Papa," Jeremy asked, "what kind of war is this, anyhow? Is this the kind of war we learned about in school that freed America from England? Is this a war to make us independent like a revolutionary war?"

"Well, Son," said his father, "that's a good question. This war is called many things. Some call it a Civil War, which is a war between two parts of the same country. But some people call it a War Between the States, some call

Jeremy went to his father first, to ask about the conflict people were calling the Civil War.

it a War of Secession, some call it the War of Northern Aggression, and yes, some call it a War of Independence. Maybe it is a revolution, but I reckon you'll just have to hear the whole story and make up your own mind.

"This is how it all began. You see, for many years, Southern states like Mississippi and Alabama and Georgia and some of us here in Virginia, have had large plantations and farms that grow cotton and tobacco and rice and sugar and we used slaves brought over here from Africa to do the work. Some of these plantations were big, so big that the owners couldn't pay enough people to work the crops. These plantations needed so many workers that the slaves were very necessary in order to plant and weed and harvest the crops. The slaves were cheap labor and besides there weren't enough white settlers in the South to do all the work that had to be done . So it was kind of a way of life here in the South and when a plantation or farm owner died, he just passed on his land and slaves to his sons and family. You see, Jeremy, the plantation owner had spent a lot of money to buy his slaves and didn't want to lose what he figured he owned.

"You know, your friend Willie is a slave and so is his daddy and so is his granddaddy and so on."

"I never really thought about that before, Papa," said Jeremy. "I just thought that Willie was a Negro so he was a slave and I was white so I wasn't, and that masters took care of slaves like you took care of me, and I never knew things could be different."

"Well," continued his father, "some folks in the North and even some in the South began to think that things should be different.

"You see, Son, the people who live in the northern states, have a different kind of life. They mostly have businesses that make things like iron and shoes and shirts and other things that don't require many workers. They hire people to do the work and they say that we who live in the Southern states should do the same. They think we should free all the slaves and hire them to do all this work.

"So in order to keep both parts of the country happy, the United States government in Washington had agreed on a kind of compromise or an agreement, that half of the states who wanted to join the United States of America (which they called the Union) could join as free states and the other half could join as slave states. They thought that if there was half of one kind and half of another, one kind couldn't control the other. That meant that everyone who lived in a free state would be considered a free person and those who lived in a slave state could own slaves and could buy or sell them—just like they bought or sold their other property.

"That worked for awhile, but then many people in the North and even some in the South began to talk and write about the need to get rid of slavery. Those people were called Abolitionists because the word 'abolish' means to get rid of something. Of course, to the people in the South, this talk meant that they would have to change the way they ran their plantations and the way they did business. Those Southern residents didn't think that the people in the northern states had any right to tell them how to run their lives and so some of them began to talk about secession. That means they would vote to take their state out of the Union, elect their own government, and be independent of the United States of America. They believed in states' rights, wherein a state could make its own laws instead of following laws made by the United States of America.

"Finally, all the talk got stronger and when the new president, elected in 1860, was a man from the political party that included the Abolitionists, some people in the South decided it was time to leave the Union. South Carolina was the first state to do this. Its residents voted to leave the Union and they elected their own government. Then they sent their own state army to Fort Sumter, a port at Charleston, to take over the fort and its armaments. Since it was in South Carolina, the people felt it belonged to South Carolina. But the United States army that was stationed there refused to give it up, and so the army of South Carolina fired shots on the fort and soldiers. This was

Fort Sumter in South Carolina is where the Civil War fighting began.

considered the beginning of the war. The date was April 12, 1861.

"When other Southern states heard of South Carolina's actions, some decided to leave the Union too. Mississippi, Florida, Alabama, Georgia, Louisiana, and Texas voted to leave the Union.

"But the new President, Abraham Lincoln, believed his duty was to keep America united as one country and did not want some of the states to leave the Union. He felt it was his duty to preserve the Constitution which was the agreement signed when the United States of America was formed. You see, America was the first nation to be ruled by the people, as a democracy. All other nations were ruled by kings or queens or czars and Lincoln did not want this democracy to break apart and fail. So he called for 75,000 volunteers to increase the size of the army and be ready to defend the Union against armies from the Southern states that would fight to leave the Union. When the Southern states heard this, they decided it was a declaration of war and others seceded or left the Union. They were Tennessee, North Carolina, Arkansas, and Virginia.

"The eleven states who voted to leave the Union called themselves a confederation of states that would each have their own government and make their own rules, the Confederate States of America. They chose a president named Jefferson Davis (who was born in Kentucky, just like President Lincoln) and they made their capital at Montgomery, Alabama. Four months later, they moved the capital to Richmond, here in our own state of Virginia.

"Now, of the thirty four states that used to be the United States of America, we have eleven in the Confederacy who want to break up the United States and twenty three in the Union states that would fight to keep the Union whole. There are twenty three million people in the North against only nine million in the South and of those nine million, five million are white and four million are black slaves."

"Well, Papa," said Jeremy after a long sigh, "that sounds like we are in for a lot of fighting. I think I'll go talk to Willie and to Jonathan and see what they think about all of this."

H E HOPPED DOWN OFF THE STOOL where he had been sitting, and ran out to find his cousin, Jonathan. He would have to wait until after supper to talk to Willie, who was out working in the fields during the daytime.

Jeremy ran into Jonathan's bedroom as the seventeen year old was packing.

"Is this what you will be taking when you go to war?" said Jeremy.

"Yes, little cousin, " said Jonathan. "When I get to the Confederate headquarters here in Virginia, they will give me a greyish-brown uniform, and a muzzle loading single shot musket with a bayonet. They will also give me a canteen for water and a tin cup for cooking and eating my food. And I will get a blanket roll to sleep on and ammunition for my gun. And I believe I'll add my harmonica. Music will be important when we're not fighting."

"Does everyone get the same thing?" questioned Jeremy.

"Almost," answered Jonathan, "except in the North, where their uniforms are blue."

"But Jonathan," said his cousin, "why do you want to go? Couldn't you just let other people settle this business of being in the Union or not being in the Union?"

"Because," said Jonathan, "I am very proud to be a Southerner and I want to protect my state and the Southern way of life. I am so proud of the way our Confederate soldiers have fought, but the war has been going on for more than a year now, and many of our soldiers have been killed and they need replacements. The North has more soldiers than we do because they have more people. If everyone in the South let someone else do the fighting, we wouldn't have enough soldiers and the South would lose!

"Since I have some time before I have to leave, let me tell you about some of the battles and how the South has fought so well. You know, we might not have as many soldiers as they do in the North, but we have great military leaders and they really know how to win battles!

"After the people of South Carolina fired the shot on Fort Sumter and got the war started, the people who lived in the North thought it would be a short fight. They thought that it was just a small rebellion. In fact some of the people who lived in Washington followed the Union soldiers to the first battle, just to watch. They thought the North would win and the fighting would be over quickly.

"But they were in for a surprise! The first real battle that took place was at Manassas, in northern Virginia. The Union army called it the battle of Bull Run because that was the name of a small creek near the railroad junction of Manassas. They were likely to name a battle after a creek or stream, while our side usually called the battle by the name of the nearest town. It happened in July of 1861. Our military leader was a man named General Thomas Jackson. His nickname was 'Stonewall' because people said he stood against the Union soldiers like a stone wall! He led our soldiers to a great victory over the Union troops, and the Union soldiers turned and ran back to Washington. More Union soldiers were killed in that battle than Confederate ones and the Confederate army was very confident. Some of the people who came just to watch, were also killed by the guns. They were silly to accompany soldiers who were going to fight!

"When the Union soldiers retreated to Washington, the North was shocked and humiliated that the South had beaten the Union forces so badly. President Lincoln appointed a new general to head the Union forces. His name was General George McClellan and he was supposed to be good at planning battles and training men. In fact, many people later said he liked to plan the battles more than he liked to fight them.

"Then came more battles. Most took place in the South and many were won by the South. But then there was a big battle in April of 1862 at Shiloh, at Pittsburg Landing on the Tennessee River in Tennessee. The Confederate soldiers made a surprise attack on the Union army, which was not at all prepared and it looked like the South might win. But then some reinforce-

Jeremy learned that the Confederate armies, led by great generals such as General Stonewall Jackson, won many of the early battles, including the battles of Manassas and Shiloh. But as the war continued, both sides began to feel exhausted and weary.

ments from the North came, and turned the tide of the battle against the South. The South eventually lost and the leader who led our forces in that battle, General Albert Sidney Johnston, was shot in the leg and bled to death. That battle lasted two days and more than 20,000 men from both sides were killed, wounded, or captured."

"You see, Jeremy," said his cousin, "a few things began to happen that meant the good commanders and the strong will of the fighting men were not enough to win a battle.

"The Union navy has begun to close off all ports along the Atlantic coast so our soldiers cannot get reinforcements of food and clothing and ammunition from the ships that usually bring new supplies to the port cities. In the North, there are many manufacturing plants that make weapons. But in the South, we have fewer manufacturing plants and have to buy many weapons from England and other countries. That's why the ports are so important to us. And we can't sell our cotton to England when the ports are closed, so we can't get the money we need to buy new supplies for our troops.

"Also, in the North, they have many good railroad lines so they can re-supply their soldiers very well. But in the South, our railroads are not as numerous or efficient. One state's railroad tracks do not match another state's tracks so we cannot send one railroad car across state lines. Instead, supplies have to be transferred by hand at every state line.

"All these things put the South at a disadvantage. That's why I see that the South really needs me and so I am going to see what I can do to help. But I promise to send letters to you to let you know about the battles and let you know what I see.

"Take care, little cousin," said Jonathan. "I'll try to win this war so you won't have to go and fight!"

With that the two shook hands and then hugged each other. Jeremy hoped Jonathan couldn't see the tear rolling down his cheek.

It was August of 1862.

2

After supper that night, Jeremy went to see his friend Willie. Jeremy learned that Willie's uncles and cousins had run away from their masters to fight for the North. Willie said that the slaves wanted the North to win the war because that would free all of the slaves. He told Jeremy that some slave owners were good to their slaves but others were awfully mean. Willie's sister was sold to one slave master, and her husband was sold to another slave master, and her little baby was taken from her arms and no one knew what had happened to that baby. His sister's slave master was very hard on his slaves, Willie told Jeremy. That slave master beat his slaves when they disobeyed him.

"My mamma cries about my sister all the time," said Willie.

Willie said he would like to be free so he wouldn't have to work all day in the fields and could go to school and learn to read.

"Willie," Jeremy said, "I could teach you how to read."

But Willie told him it was forbidden to teach slaves how to read and both of them would get a beating if anyone found out.

Jeremy was surprised at himself for not thinking about these things before. He hadn't thought about buying and selling people like you'd buy and sell a horse. And he hadn't thought about how terrible it would be to have his family split up and sold to mean people. He figured that the people who wanted to get rid of slavery had probably been thinking about all these things for a long time.

As the war continued, life in the North and the South got harder, but there were more hardships in the South since so many men went to fight for the Confederacy and left all the chores to the women and children. Also, since so many of the battles were fought on Southern land, the crops were being destroyed and food was getting scarce.

Jeremy and his mother heard stories about the terrible battles and he waited anxiously to receive news from Jonathan. But the first letter from his cousin didn't arrive until December of 1862.

Dear Jeremy,

This war is worse than I ever imagined.

Remember I told you about the battle at Manassas, which the North called Bull Run? Well, when I arrived in August, they sent me there to fight the second battle of Bull Run. I'm proud to say that the South won.

But while I was fighting next to one of our neighbors, a shell hit him and blew off part of his leg. There is no hospital here, but they converted one of the large homes into a place where we carry the wounded. I stopped by to see him and saw that they had cut off the rest of his leg. Infection had set in and there was no way to stop it from killing him without taking the leg. There's no medicine that can stop infection. I have seen so many soldiers missing legs and arms. In fact, I have seen arms and legs all by themselves, piled up on the battlefield where they were blown off of the men or were amputated.

But I'm not discouraged. The South is fighting well and that win at Manassas was a good one.

In September, we fought in Maryland. We have a great leader, General Robert E. Lee. He wanted to take control of the Union's weapons supply located at Harper's Ferry, so he split his forces to accomplish his goals and sent written orders to his officers to let them know of his plans. We did take Harper's Ferry, but one copy of the orders was dropped by accident and found by a soldier from the North. This tipped off the North about our locations. We met the Union troops around Sharpsburg, Maryland, at Antietam Creek.

The battle lasted only one day but 23,000 men were severely

General Robert E. Lee was the Confederate general who Jonathan described as a "great leader" in his letter to Jeremy.

Jonathan wrote that during the battle of Antietam, called the bloodiest one-day battle of the war, soldiers sometimes even killed each other with bayonets.

wounded and 4,800 of them died right there on the field. Many others died later of infection. If you can imagine seeing 4,800 dead bodies and thousands lying on a field, badly hurt, you know what it was like. We had only 40,000 troops from the South fighting 87,000 troops from the North. The army here called it the bloodiest one-day battle they had ever seen. Some of the soldiers killed each other with bayonets. That's a terrible thing to see. The battle was a draw between the North and the South.

Then in December, we went onto Fredericksburg in Virginia on the Potomac River and fought with the Union soldiers again and this time we won. Thank the Lord!

President Lincoln replaced his General McClellan, because he was not taking advantage of opportunities to fight. President Lincoln seems to have a hard time finding the kind of military leaders like the South's Stonewall Jackson and Robert E. Lee.

I've learned a few things in this war about men. Some of the ones you think will be strong, might be cowards, and some you figure will be weak, turn out to be strong fighters. Some of them fight honorably and some are just plain mean and might stab someone who is already wounded. We are called Rebels or Graycoats. And they call our Confederate flag the Rebel flag. We call the Northerners, Yankees or Federals or Bluecoats. Their flag is the Stars and Stripes that used to be our flag. I also learned that most of us from the South joined up as volunteers, but the soldiers from the North were required to fight and some were paid to join. They call that conscription, when you tell a man that he has to fight for his country. Some of our Southern boys are starting to be conscripted also, because we need so many soldiers for this war.

You know, little cousin, that the Confederates can't win every battle against all the soldiers that they have in the Union army. But if we can at least convince the North that we will fight well and never give up on what we believe, then maybe we can convince them to leave us alone and let us secede from their Union.

Well, I will close this now and I'll write again as soon as I get the chance.

Your cousin,

Jonathan

Jeremy read the letter five times, then put it into his Bible for safekeeping.

3

Christmas was coming, but it would not be the festive occasion he remembered. His father and many uncles had joined Jonathan, fighting in the army of the South. And his granddaddy and uncles from Kentucky wouldn't be with them this year, because they had gone to fight for the North.

Since so many of the slaves had run up north to freedom or to fight in the war, and all the young white boys and men were off fighting in the war, Jeremy and his mom and sisters had to take care of the plantation and rebuild things that were broken. Willie and his family did not run away, but stayed and helped Jeremy and his mom and sisters.

When Southern troops came through the fields, the whole family had to get food ready for them and help them if they were sick or wounded. Jeremy's mom sewed clothing for neighbors in exchange for flour and items she couldn't grow or buy and she sewed uniforms for the soldiers. Sometimes she received payment for the uniforms but often there was no money to pay her. Some of Jeremy's girl cousins had gone to help care for the wounded soldiers. All summer and fall, Jeremy had worked in the fields just like Willie. He learned first hand what it was like to work that hard. There were no new clothes, and very little time to play. School was cancelled due to the shortage of teachers and because the families needed the children at home to help with chores. Schoolhouses were turned into hospitals for the soldiers.

Sometimes, a neighbor would bring a newspaper, and everyone would gather around the table to read and hear about the war.

A famous writer, Walt Whitman, was following some of the troops and wrote stories of the war. He told of being in a Maryland hospital in which two men were lying, wounded, in separate rooms. One had been fighting for a Confederate regiment and had a leg amputated, but it was infected. He was nineteen. The other soldier had been fighting for the Union forces and was severely wounded. He was seventeen. Both grew up in the same home in Maryland because they were brothers. Both died within days of each other.

It seemed to be a war of brothers against brothers and friends against friends.

Jeremy and his mother heard from their Kentucky cousins that one incident certainly proved this. A group of Kentucky soldiers fighting for the Confederacy were weary after a day of marching through Kentucky hills. They spotted a barn, and after checking to make sure it was empty, decided to camp there for the night. They slept in the hay loft to make sure they would not be detected. During the night, they heard a group of soldiers enter that same barn. One of the Confederate soldiers recognized the voice of his brother among the voices of the newly arrived soldiers, but he knew his brother was fighting for the North. The two fighting units, who were enemies by day, greeted each other that night and shared battle stories. When dawn arrived, they shook hands and went their separate ways.

CHILDREN WERE PART OF THIS WAR. One newspaper story told of a child from Ohio who was only ten years old when he ran away from home to serve in a Michigan unit to fight for the North. The young boys usually served as drummer boys, who played to encourage the soldiers as they marched into battle, or signaled to stop fighting or to reload weapons and charge again. Other boys were buglers whose music woke the soldiers or told them it was time to sleep.

But some really were soldiers. One story told of a young boy who was only twelve when he was wounded as his left hand and arm were shattered by a shell. He was considered the youngest soldier to be wounded in the war. Most soldiers were eighteen or nineteen years old. Half of the men were younger than twenty-four.

Jeremy heard these stories with a heavy heart. He worried about his cousin and his papa and his uncles. He asked his mom about the mail every day, but the next letter from Jonathan didn't come until the end of 1863 and it told Jeremy more than he really wanted to know about war.

Dear Jeremy,

Well, it's been a whole year and I have been fighting so much and trying to keep cool in the summer and warm in the winter and find enough food to eat. But I finally got time to let you know how things are going.

President Lincoln found a great general in a man named Ulysses S. Grant, and he is leading many of the battles.

There have been so many of them, that I don't know where to begin. I'll just tell you about the biggest ones now, and I'll tell you about the others when I get home.

In May of this year, 1863, we fought at Chancellorsville and we won. But some of our great military leaders are getting killed. Stonewall Jackson was mortally wounded and died. We are already outnumbered because there are many more soldiers in the North, so it is very important for us to have good leaders. Losing General Jackson was a terrible blow.

Then in July, some of our Southern armies fought at Vicksburg, Mississippi, on the Mississippi River. The North won and things began to look bad for us because the North was able to control the Mississippi River and we couldn't get food or supplies from the river boats.

Another thing happened in July of this year, 1863. General Lee had hoped to drive us up to Harrisburg, Pennsylvania, to capture the B & O Railroad and cut off supplies to the North and threaten the Union capital of Washington. You see, we heard that many people in the North were getting fed up with the war lasting so long and being so bloody, and many were ready to give in and let the Southern states secede after all. If

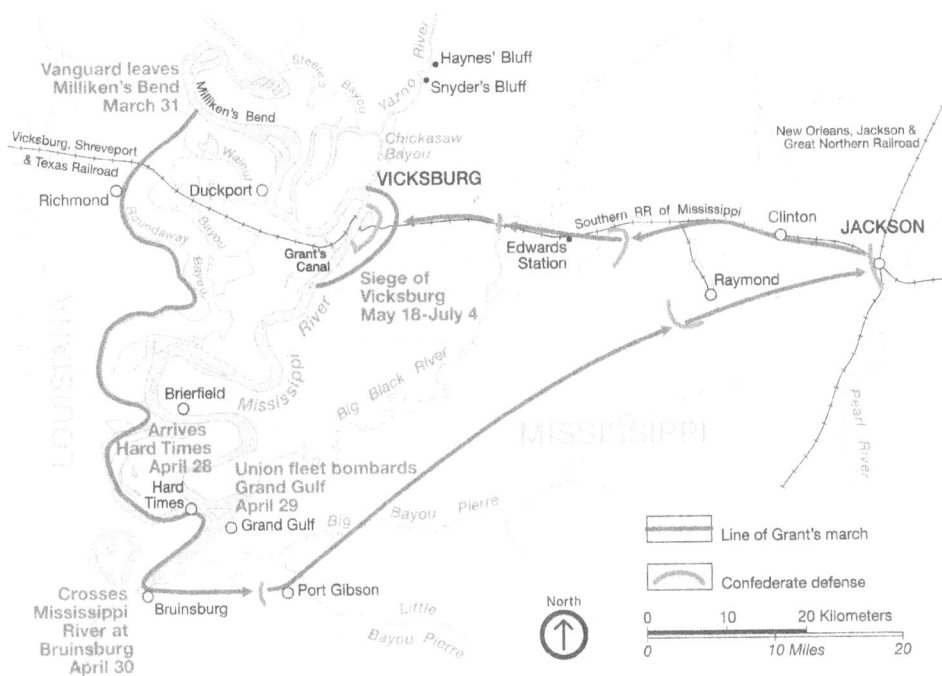

This map shows the location of the Battle of Vicksburg, which Jonathan described as important because it gave the North control of the Mississippi River.

WHAT KIND OF WAR WAS IT, ANYHOW?

people saw that we could cut off their supplies, maybe they would decide not to re-elect Lincoln and let us secede. Then maybe we could get out of this United States and get back to living the kind of lifestyle we want to live in the South.

But a strange thing happened while we were planning to go to Harrisburg. One of our officers sent a unit of his soldiers into the small town of Gettysburg, Pennsylvania, to get boots for his soldiers. We are not only having a hard time getting food, we also wear out boots and can't get replacements. In fact, I have seen our soldiers taking boots off of dead soldiers from both sides, just so they could have something for their feet!

When the soldiers were in Gettysburg, some Union soldiers saw them, and from that meeting, began a major battle of the war. The battle lasted three days. The first day, we pushed the Union army up to an area called Cemetery Ridge. But during the night, they received replacement forces plus several cannons. When our troops approached them the next day, the cannon shots killed many of our soldiers. That was a bloody battle and we lost one/third of our army and we were not able to reach our goal. Things began to look bad. Some called the battle at Gettysburg the turning point of the war, because we lost so many soldiers. I guess losing at Gettysburg and then losing use of the Mississippi River when we lost Vicksburg make things look bad for our side.

Then in the fall, there were important battles around Chattanooga, Tennessee. Chattanooga is important because of railroad lines and rivers that can carry replacements for our Confederate troops. Our armies felt we would win because we were located on Lookout Mountain and Missionary Ridge surrounding the Union forces in the valley below. We hoped to starve them out. But they received reinforcements and they charged up the mountain and ridge and took over those areas.

After that, the Union's General William T. Sherman began to march into Georgia, burning everything as he went, to prevent the Confederate soldiers from getting food and supplies from the people in Georgia. He destroyed Atlanta and then marched to the coast at Savannah. But then he went up to Columbia, South Carolina, and burned that town, too.

I have seen a lot of former slaves fighting for the North. We have slaves with us too, but they build camps and cook and they are not soldiers.

We don't have much to eat here. We mainly eat uncooked corn that we pick up from the fields. Sometimes we cook the corn and some soldiers catch rats and mice in the fields and cook and eat them. I haven't tried that yet. The water often tastes bad, and everyone has diarrhea and lice.

How I wish I could be back home eating some of those good sweet potatoes and fried chicken and biscuits that Willie's mammy knows how to make.

I'll write again when I get a chance.

Your cousin,

Jonathan

Jeremy was glad he didn't have to tell his cousin that there were no sweet potatoes and chicken anymore. Everyone at home was eating beans and corn and anything they could find.

He also was glad he didn't have to tell his cousin that part of their state of Virginia, up in the northwest, had voted to separate themselves from the rest of Virginia and become a free state that was called West Virginia. Those people lived in hilly areas with coal mines and other businesses and they did not need slaves because they did not have large plantations that required many workers. They disagreed with their Southern neighbors about seceding from the Union.

Jeremy and his mother continued to read and hear about the battles. Some of them took place so close to home that the neighbors told them

Jeremy and his mother learned that President Lincoln found a great leader in General Ulysses S. Grant and put him in charge of all Union forces.

about what happened. They learned that even though the South won many battles, the North was beginning to win most of them. President Lincoln had found a great leader in General Ulysses S. Grant and had put him in charge of all Union forces. His strategy was to encircle the Confederate troops and bring an end to the war.

Jeremy and his mom learned that in May and June of 1864, there were battles in an area called the Wilderness and at Spotslvania and at Cold Harbor in Virginia. The forest caught fire from some of the shooting in the Wilderness area, and some soldiers died in the fire.

Then at Petersburg, near Richmond, Virginia, General Lee and General Grant and their armies battled for nine months. Finally the Southern forces retreated to Lynchburg. This abandoned the Confederate capital of Richmond to the Union forces. And on April 9, 1865, General Robert E. Lee surrendered to General Ulysses S. Grant at the Appomattox Court House in Richmond, Virginia.

THE BLOODY WAR WAS OVER. It had lasted exactly four years. More than 350,000 Northern men had died and more than 250,000 Southern men died. More than 180,000 former black slaves and freed black men fought for the North. They fought very hard and very well according to many reports. In fact, all the soldiers on both sides fought very well, despite great hardships. Some battles were won by leadership and strategy by the generals, but some battles were won by the sheer determination and endurance of the soldiers. They were each fighting to preserve a way of life that they valued dearly. These men were not trained to be soldiers, but were farm boys and shopkeepers who learned about soldiering out in the field. Many of them died from battle wounds, but many died from disease or dysentery and some even starved to death.

The war proved, as Lincoln had hoped, that America could continue to be a Union, governed by its citizens, and stronger as one united country than

President Abraham Lincoln had worked to make sure that the United States of America could continue to be one nation.

it would have been if it had been divided.

Jeremy's dad came home and so did Jonathan. But Jonathan was on crutches because he had lost his right leg to a battle wound. He would never be the same. He had seen so many men die on both sides of the war. He had seen the best side of men and the worst side of them. In fact, it was just after he had bent down to give a dying soldier from the North a drink from his water canteen, when the ungrateful soldier shot Jonathan in the leg. He was not Jeremy's fun-loving young cousin anymore. He was a wounded man of twenty, embittered by a vicious war.

The South had lost more than the war. Almost all of the battles had been fought in the South so that most of the land was destroyed and needed so much rebuilding to grow anything again.

President Lincoln signed a presidential proclamation called the Emancipation Proclamation in 1863. It granted freedom to the slaves that were in the states that voted to secede from the Union. But the Proclamation only applied to the portions of those states that were occupied by Union troops because the other portions of the Confederacy did not accept rules set down by the Federal Government. Some of the freed slaves stayed on and worked for their former masters and some went up North to find work.

Life was difficult for everyone. The South had to rebuild its homes, plantations, and land. But the North had a large war debt and had to begin to tax its citizens to pay for the war. The Union established a Freedman's Bureau to help the newly freed slaves with food and education. Northern soldiers arrived in the South in 1867 to guarantee freedom to the slaves and they stayed ten years. Ultimately, the 13th Amendment to the United States Constitution was approved. It forbids slavery everywhere in the United States.

Abraham Lincoln had hoped to bring a peaceful end to the war and ease the burden for the South, but he was assassinated while he and his wife, Mary, were watching a play at a theatre in Washington. His killer was a man named John Wilkes Booth who blamed the President for causing the war.

In Lincoln's absence, the United States government enacted tough penalties on the South and called it Reconstruction. It divided the Confederacy into five military districts. Each state would have to conform to strict rules in order to become a member of the United States again. Each state would have to create a new constitution fashioned after the United States' constitution and give up slavery, and declare all men free and allow all men over twenty-one to vote. At the time of the war's end, the Southern states did not have governments, or courts, or police. And a whole generation of men between seventeen and thirty was either dead or severely wounded.

Some people from the North came to the South to help out as teachers. But some Northerners came to take advantage of the struggling Southerners. They charged high prices for goods they brought to sell, and were called carpetbaggers because they carried their goods in bags that looked like they were made of carpet material. That word has come to mean someone who tries to take advantage of someone else.

Jeremy and his father and family never spoke to his granddaddy and cousins in Kentucky again. Some families in the states that bordered the line between the North and South refused to forgive family members who fought for the side that they opposed. Some families mended their differences, but some did not.

People in the South learned that slavery could not continue and that the war was the wrong way to solve the differences between the North and the South.

"So, Jeremy," said his father after he had begun to build his farm and land again, "did you decide what kind of war it was?"

"Well, Papa," said Jeremy as he helped his father build a new fence, "when I read in my school book that the word civil means civilized and within the law and orderly and peaceable and with consideration for others, I can't believe that the war was any of those things. I really believe it was . . ."

4

Jeremy learned about a war that had different meanings in the eyes of many people. Some believed it was a war for the South's independence. Some felt it would break up the United States into two countries. Slaves believed it would bring them freedom. And some thought it was a revolt against Northern oppression of the South.

To answer his papa's question, here are some of the things Jeremy might have said:

"I really believe it was a War of Independence because I believe the South wanted to be independent from the United States of America because they believed it was controlled by persons from the North."

or

"I believe it was a Revolutionary War because the South really was revolting against the North and wanted to be free from their control."

or

"I really believe it was the War Between the States because the South was fighting for their way of life and the North was fighting for its way of life."

or

"I believe it was a War of Secession because the South really did want to secede or leave the United States of America and form their own country and carry out their own way of doing business."

As a reader of this book, do you agree with any of these answers? Do you have a different idea? What would you have said?

Bibliography

An Encyclopedia of World History, William L. Langer, ed., Houghton Mifflin Co., 1952

Barnes, Eric Wollencott, *The War Between The States*, Whittlesey House, McGraw Hill, 1959

Battle Chronicles of the Civil War, James M. McPherson, ed., Macmillan Publishing, 1989

Black, Robert C. III, *The Railroads of The Confederacy*, Chapel Hill, University of North Carolina Press, 1952

Blackerby, H.C., *Blacks in Blue and Grey*, Portals Press, Tuscaloosa Press, 1979

Brother Against Brother, A Time-Life Book, Prentiss Hall Press, 1990

Carter, Alden R., *The Civil War: American Tragedy*, Franklin Watts Library Edition, 1992

Copeland, Peter F., *Story of The Civil War Coloring Book*, Dover Publications, 1991

Davis, William C., *The Orphan Brigade" the Kentucky Confederates Who Couldn't Go Home*, Doubleday & Co ., 1988

"Diary of Company Aytch," a video by Samuel Watkins, 1994

Encyclopedia Americana, A.H. McDannald, ed., Americana Corp., 1946

Foote, Shelby, *The Civil War: A Narrative*, Vol I, Random House, 1958

Freeman, Douglas Southwall, *Lee's Lieutenants*, Vol. I, Charles Schribner's Sons, 1942

Hakim, Joy, *History of US: Reconstruction and Reform*, Oxford University Press, 1994

Hakim, Joy, *History of US: War Terrible War*, Oxford University Press, 1994

"Illuminating Antietam," Les Thomas, Southern Living, December, 1999

Jackman, John S., *Diary of a Confederate Soldier*, University of South Carolina Press, 1998

McCarthy, Agnes and Reddick, Laurence, *Worth Fighting For*, Zenith Books, Doubleday, 1965

Macdonald, John, *Great Battles of the Civil War*, Macmillian Publishing Co., 1988

Moore, Kay, *If You Lived at the Time of the Civil War*, Scholastic Inc., 1994

Murphy, Tom, *The Boys' War*, Clarion Books, 1998

Pratt, Fletcher, *The Civil War*, Garden City Books., 1955

Price, William H., *Civil War Handbook*, L.B. Prince Co. Inc., 1961

Priest, John Michael, *Antietum: The Soldiers' Battle*, Oxford University Press, 1989

Stiles, T.J., *In Their Own Words: Civil War Commanders*, Berkley Publishing Group, 1995

Straubling, Harold Elk, *Civil War: Eyewitness Reports*, Archon Books, 1985

Stowe, Harriet Beecher, *Uncle Tom's Cabin*, Bantam Books, 1851

Vandiver, Frank E., *Blood Brothers*, Texas A & M University Press, 1992

Werner, Emmy E., *Reluctant Witnesses*, Westview Press, 1998

Whitman, Walt, *Walt Whitman's Civil War*, Alfred A. Knopf, 1960

Acknowledgments

My advisors on this book included:

My grandson, Brett Ekberg, who is now twelve years old and lives in Pennsylvania.

John Clements, a member of the Society for the Study of the Great Battles and Major Skirmishes of the Civil War and member of the Association for the Preservation of Civil War Sites, Inc., who lives in Birmingham.

Kay Wheeler, a Civil War enthusiast who was raised in Kentucky.

Bob Watson, a Civil War enthusiast who grew up in West Virginia.

And Lesley Stahl, a fourteen-year-old girl who is a Civil War enthusiast and lives in Huntington Beach, California.